THIS CANDLEWICK BOOK BELONGS TO

• •

• •

• •

For Mum and Dad

Expert Consultant: Stuart Atkinson

Because NASA uses feminine pronouns when referring to ships of exploration and spacecraft,
such as *Curiosity*, the author has elected to follow their style for this book.

First U.S. edition 2018
This edition published specially for KiwiCo 2020 by Candlewick Press

Library of Congress Catalog Card Number 2018935023
ISBN 978-0-7636-9504-0 (Candlewick trade edition)
ISBN 978-1-5362-1748-3 (KiwiCo edition)

20 APS 1

Printed in Humen, Dongguan, China

This book was typeset in Nevis.
The illustrations were done in mixed media.

Candlewick Press
99 Dover Street
Somerville, Massachusetts 02144

visit us at www.candlewick.com

CURIOSITY
The Story of a Mars Rover

MARKUS MOTUM

CANDLEWICK PRESS

**Wherever you are in the world right now,
I'm a very long way away.
I'm not even on the same planet as you.**

I'm a Mars rover. A rover is a moving robot, built to explore far-off places—

places too far away or dangerous for humans to visit.

How did I get here? Why was I sent?

This is my story.

Humans have always wondered about Earth and its place in the universe. Although scientists have made great discoveries and explained some of the mysteries of space, the planets hold their secrets well. Many questions remain unanswered. Of these, one question intrigues humans above all others:

Is there anybody else out there?

Scientists decided that the best place to look for other life
was on one of our closest neighboring planets . . .

MARS,
the red planet.

In addition to being one of our two closest neighboring planets, Mars is the planet in our solar system that's most similar to Earth. Scientists think that in the past, Mars may have had environments similar to ones on Earth today. Mars is covered in red dust now, but there is evidence that millions of years ago, the planet may have had lakes, flowing rivers, and even great oceans.

Why does this matter?

Because on Earth, water is a necessity for life!

However, there is one problem. . . .

The trip to Mars in a spacecraft can be over

350,0

00,000

miles long.

That's 350 million miles (560 million kilometers), a distance much, much farther than any human has ever traveled in space. Even with our modern technology, we don't have a practical way to get humans to Mars—the journey would take at least six months—or to get them back.

Humans have been able to explore closer to home. On July 20, 1969, *Apollo 11* landed on the Moon. Astronaut Neil Armstrong took one famous step and became the first person to set foot there. For the few hours he and Buzz Aldrin walked on its surface, people could look up at the Moon and know that someone might be looking back at them.

Mars is about two hundred times farther from Earth than the Moon, a journey that is currently very difficult for humans to undertake. The red planet is also an inhospitable environment. But what if it were possible to send an explorer who didn't need food, water, or oxygen? That's where I come in.

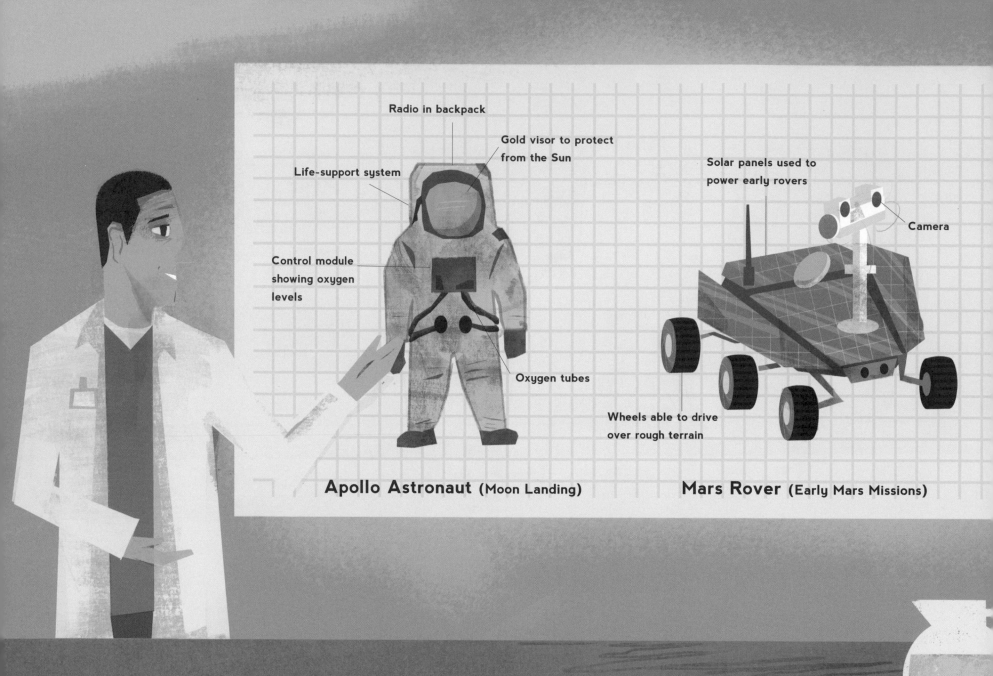

Radio in backpack

Gold visor to protect
from the Sun

Life-support system

Control module
showing oxygen
levels

Oxygen tubes

Apollo Astronaut (Moon Landing)

Solar panels used to
power early rovers

Camera

Wheels able to drive
over rough terrain

Mars Rover (Early Mars Missions)

Scientists at NASA (the National Aeronautics and Space Administration) came up with the idea to send robots to Mars in humans' place. The robots would need to be able to move over rough terrain with all the equipment needed to collect data and samples.

So the scientists began to design rovers like me.

The project to build and design Mars rovers was—and still is—based at the Jet Propulsion Laboratory, near Los Angeles, California. I needed to be larger and more advanced than any of the rovers NASA had built before.

Previous successful rovers had taken photos of Mars, giving NASA never-before-
seen images. Other missions were "orbiters" and "flybys"—flying around
or past Mars to gather information without even landing on the planet.

By 2007, thirty-nine missions to the red planet had been launched, and over half had ended
in failure. Some of these earlier missions had become lost in space, while others crashed
into Mars, never to be heard from again.

The lab where I was built had to be kept as clean as possible.
Everyone had to wear white coveralls, which were nicknamed bunny suits.
These suits stopped dust and germs from spreading to me and my equipment.

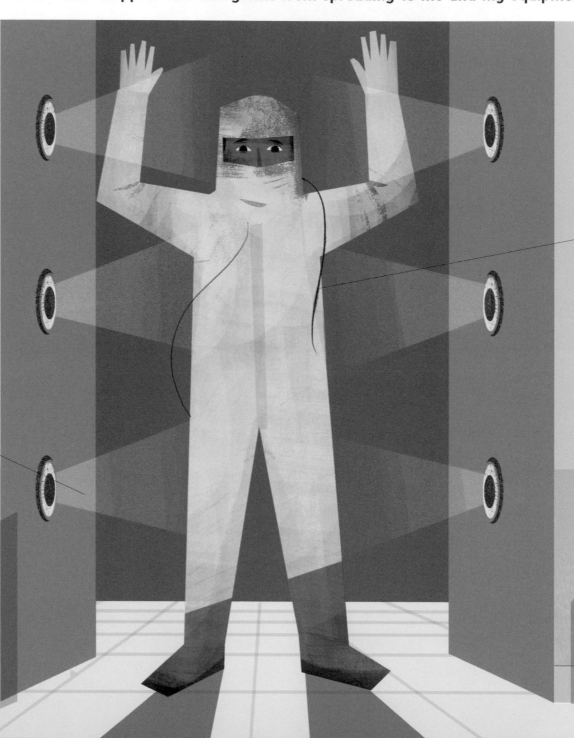

The suit covers a person from head to toe—this way no skin, hair, or other kinds of human dust will be shed into the clean room. (Humans make a lot of dust!)

This air shower blasts away dust, hair, and skin from coveralls before people enter.

Static electricity can harm equipment. This cord keeps the team member from giving off a static shock by transferring any static charges to the floor.

Filters are used to remove as much dust in the lab's air as possible.

The team didn't want to think they had discovered tiny forms of life on Mars, only to realize that it was just Earth bacteria I'd brought with me.

Scientists re-created Martian environments in test rooms at the lab so they could check that I was prepared.

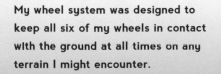

My wheel system was designed to keep all six of my wheels in contact with the ground at all times on any terrain I might encounter.

Entirely new technologies had to be invented for my mission. I needed to be able to carry a lot of equipment to test what I found on Mars—my own portable laboratory. To give the mission the best chance of being successful, years of testing were needed to make sure everything would work correctly the first time. After all, if something were to go wrong on Mars, no one could come and fix me.

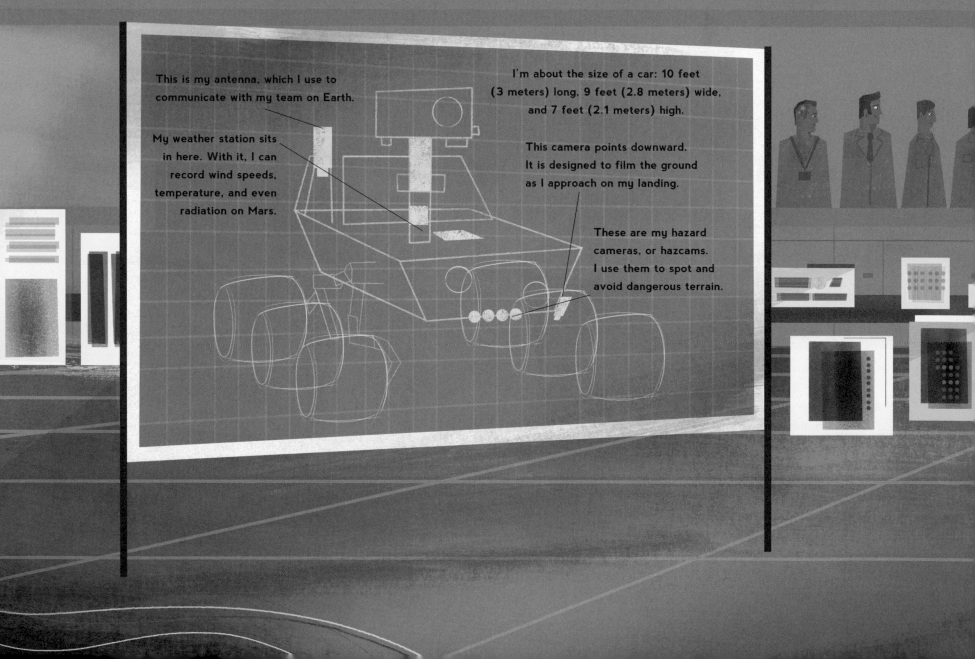

This is my antenna, which I use to communicate with my team on Earth.

My weather station sits in here. With it, I can record wind speeds, temperature, and even radiation on Mars.

I'm about the size of a car: 10 feet (3 meters) long, 9 feet (2.8 meters) wide, and 7 feet (2.1 meters) high.

This camera points downward. It is designed to film the ground as I approach on my landing.

These are my hazard cameras, or hazcams. I use them to spot and avoid dangerous terrain.

NASA ran a competition for members of the public to choose a name for me. Some of the names considered were *Adventure*, *Journey*, *Pursuit*, *Vision*, and *Wonder*. The winning entry was submitted by Clara Ma, who was a sixth-grader from Kansas. The name she picked for me was . . .

CURIOSITY.

My body carries the onboard chemistry lab where I run all my science experiments.

Just like you, I have a shoulder, elbow, and wrist—so I can be as flexible as possible.

This is my battery. It's nuclear-powered. The plutonium in here will power me for years.

My robotic hand has many tools, including a drill and a brush to probe the surface of Mars.

These wheel treads leave marks that help me judge how far I've moved.

And then I was ready to fly to Mars! It was best to launch eastward and close to the equator to get as much energy from Earth's spin as possible. This also meant it was safest to launch where the ocean was to the east, just in case something went wrong. So I had to be taken to Florida to begin my space mission. I boarded a carrier plane . . .

and flew from Los Angeles . . .

Washington

Oregon

Idaho

Montana

North Dakota

South Dakota

Wyoming

Nebraska

Nevada

Utah

Colorado

Kansas

California

JPL

Arizona

New Mexico

Oklahoma

Texas

Minnesota
Wisconsin
Maine
Vermont
New Hampshire
New York
Massachusetts
Connecticut
Iowa
Michigan
Rhode Island
Pennsylvania
New Jersey
Illinois
Ohio
Delaware
Indiana
Washington, D.C.
Maryland
West Virginia
Missouri
Kentucky
Virginia
North Carolina
Arkansas
Tennessee
South Carolina
Georgia
Mississippi
Alabama
Louisiana
Florida

to the Kennedy
Space Center.

The rocket that would take me into space was waiting for me in Florida. The *Atlas V* rocket is around 200 feet (61 meters) tall—the height of a nineteen-story building—and it is almost all rocket fuel. This is because it needs to be powerful enough to launch whatever it is carrying, known as its payload, into space.

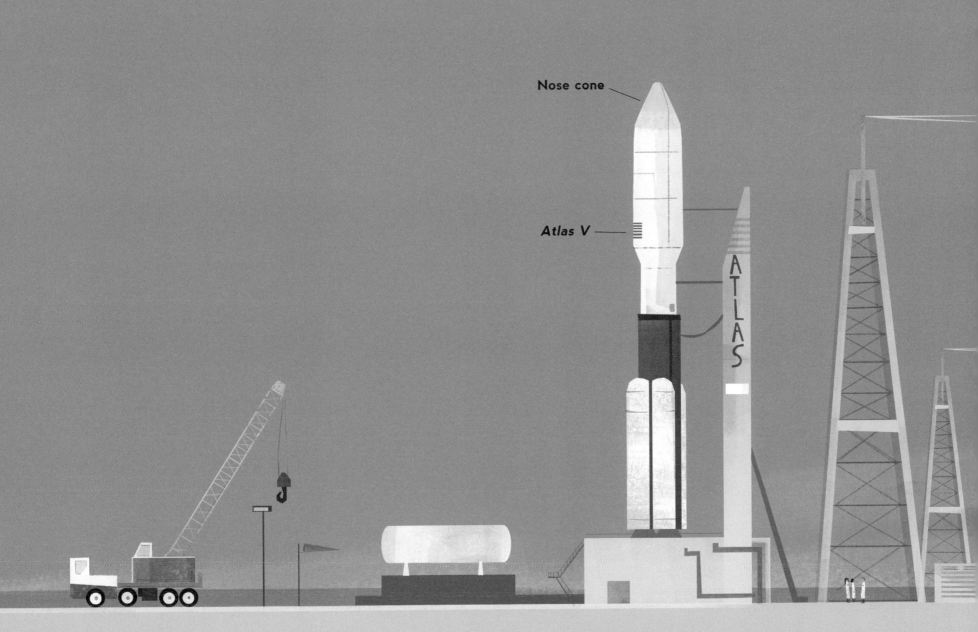

Nose cone

Atlas V

ATLAS

The *Atlas V* is known as an expendable launch vehicle, which means its parts can be used only once. I was placed inside the nose cone, at the very top. The cone is like a shield that protects the rest of the rocket as it breaks through Earth's atmosphere.

My launch date was chosen carefully so that I had the best chance at a
successful launch and the shortest trip possible. Because planets orbit the
Sun at different speeds and distances, sometimes they are far apart and
other times they are much closer together.

Saturn

Neptune

Uranus

Jupiter

Venus

Sun

Every few years, Earth and Mars are lined up so they are relatively
close, allowing missions to reach Mars more quickly and using less fuel.

If we had missed this opportunity, the mission would have been delayed for years.

Mercury

Moon

Earth

Mars

Launch day—November 26, 2011—arrived. I was ready to fly to Mars. In the control room, the team ran through the final checks.

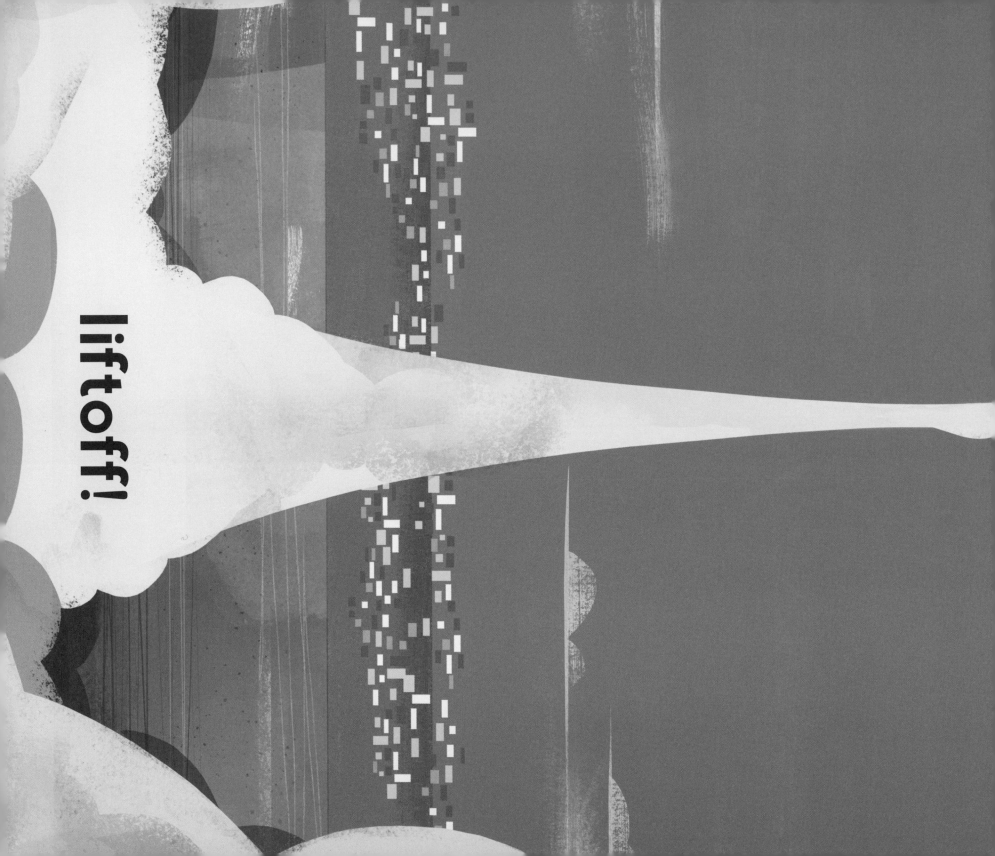

liftoff!

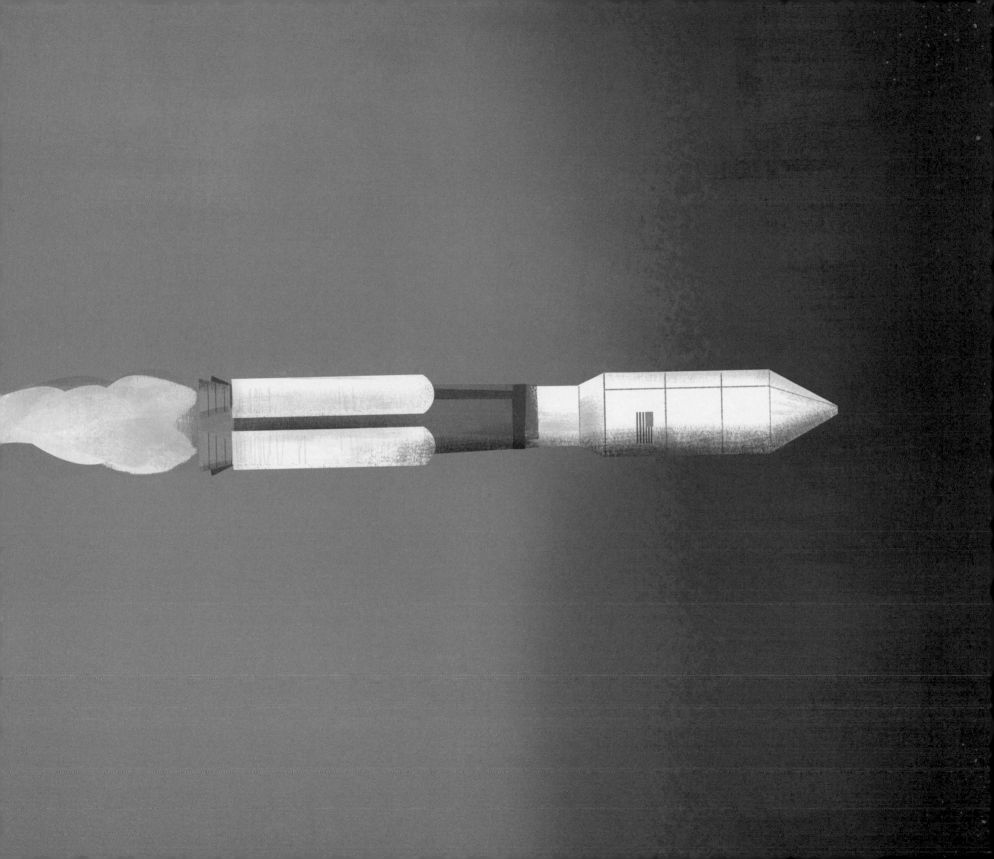

The first part of my journey was breaking through Earth's atmosphere and reaching space. Once *Atlas V's* various boosters had done their job of getting the rocket into space, they broke off and fell safely into the ocean.

This is the common core booster and its engine. It's about 107 feet (33 meters) long. Its fuel tanks were filled with kerosene and liquid oxygen.

These four boosters helped the main rocket escape Earth's gravity, then fell back to Earth once they were used up.

Once the rocket had carried me safely into space, the nose cone protecting me broke off and fell back toward Earth. Then the common core booster detached.

Next, a second, smaller engine burned its fuel to launch me out of Earth's orbit. Forty minutes after liftoff, that engine detached, and I was heading for Mars.

I made the rest of the journey in this protective shell called the module. The module used its star scanner and Sun sensor to guide itself. Thrusters on the outside of the module could change its direction when necessary. They were the only part of the rocket that made the long journey to Mars with me.

After 253 days

hurtling through space, I finally arrived near Mars, traveling 13,000 miles (21,000 kilometers) per hour! Next would be the trickiest part of my entire journey—landing safely.

Parachute

Back Shell

Entering Mars's atmosphere,
I was traveling more than 1,000 miles
(1,600 kilometers) per hour.
The metal heat shield protecting me
heated up to 3,800° F (2,100° C).

Heat Shield

The heat shield fell away, allowing
my radar to determine where I
should land. A huge parachute
slowed me down to about 200
miles (320 kilometers) per hour.

No rover or space mission had ever tried the type of landing I was programmed for. It would take seven
minutes from the time I penetrated the atmosphere around Mars until I landed on the surface. The team at
NASA called it "Seven Minutes of Terror." If I had been landing on Earth, the atmosphere would have slowed
down my entry. But Mars has much less atmosphere than our home planet, so as soon as I entered the
atmosphere, a huge parachute opened, slowing me to about 200 miles (320 kilometers) per hour.

I was now only traveling at about 2 miles (3 kilometers) per hour. About 60 feet (20 meters) above the surface, the "sky crane" cables lowered me carefully to the surface.

Powered Descent Vehicle

Cables

Once the descent vehicle sensed I was on the ground, it cut the cables and flew away so it wouldn't land on top of me!

My back shell detached, and the powered descent vehicle's retro-rockets fired. I made a sharp turn to avoid flying into the falling parachute.

I was still moving too fast, so I dropped out of the back shell, and for a few seconds I was free-falling to the ground. Suddenly the powered descent vehicle, which was holding me, fired eight rockets, slowing me down almost completely. Then I was ready to be lowered to the surface on cables, known as the "sky crane" maneuver. Once the descent vehicle detected slack in the cables, it knew I must be on the surface of Mars and released the cables.

I had made it.

As soon as I was safely on the surface, I sent a message to my NASA team letting them know that I had landed.

Because of the huge distance between Mars and Earth, the message took fifteen minutes to get back to Earth.

It was a tense time in the control room as everyone waited. Then the words everyone wanted to hear were read out:

"Touchdown confirmed. We're safe on Mars!"

It wasn't just the NASA team who had been watching my landing. All around the world, people tuned in to see if I had arrived safely after my long journey. Crowds gathered in New York's Times Square to watch on a giant screen. It was an exciting but scary time. After all, if just one thing had gone wrong, all contact between me and the team back on Earth would have been lost.

When they heard I'd landed, some people cheered—others breathed huge sighs of relief!

The next thing I did on Mars was send images of myself back to NASA to make sure I hadn't been damaged during the journey. My landing had been perfect—if a little dusty. The site had been carefully selected by scientists as a place likely to have evidence of water. Now it was time to start looking.

Since 2012, I have been exploring Mars. The NASA team looks through my seventeen cameras and chooses potential spots on the surface that may have evidence of life. Once something is identified, I move toward it. I can move more than 600 feet (200 meters) per day.

NASA also wants to understand how Mars was formed and how it has changed over time. The deeper I dig, the more information I can gather.

I drill into rocks and scoop up material. I then test it in my onboard laboratory. Gradually, by piecing together information from different locations, NASA hopes to build a picture of the planet's past and perhaps discover why Mars changed from being a warm planet with water to the cold, dry planet it is today.

Firing my laser at rocks helps NASA find out what they are made of.

As a hole is drilled, the powder gets sent up a tube into my arm. My arm then reaches over and places the powder in my laboratory for testing.

There are many questions still to be answered. What was Mars like long ago? How suitable was it for life? Did it once support any life-forms? The tests I carry out will provide as many answers as possible. Most likely, the discoveries I make will lead to more questions!

With space exploration, questions can be just as exciting as answers. Thanks to the curiosity of explorers,

Neil Armstrong's footprints are on the Moon. And now my wheel tracks are being left on another planet.

Perhaps one day soon, footprints from the next generation of explorers will leave their marks here as well.

"Curiosity is the passion that drives us through our everyday lives. We have become explorers and scientists with our need to ask questions and to wonder. We will never know everything there is to know, but with our burning curiosity, we have learned so much." —Clara Ma

MARS ROVERS

Although *Curiosity* is the most advanced rover sent to Mars so far, she is not the only rover to explore the red planet. In 1997, the *Sojourner* rover was the first to land successfully on Mars and remained active for much longer than expected; it was nearly three months before *Sojourner* sent her final transmission to Earth.

The Mars exploration rover *Spirit* was the next to make a successful landing, in 2004. She also survived much longer than she was expected to—and made the amazing discovery that there was once water on Mars. After traveling nearly five miles over five years, *Spirit* got stuck in dust and eventually lost contact with Earth.

But *Spirit*'s twin rover is still operating today. *Opportunity* landed three weeks after *Spirit*, and since then has traveled farther than the length of a marathon! No other robot has ever gone so far on the surface of another world. *Opportunity* continues to explore Mars's craters and send back images, many years after she was expected to shut down.

Where will our curiosity take us next?

NASA MARS ROVER MISSION GOALS

- Determine whether life ever arose on Mars
- Characterize the climate of Mars
- Characterize the geology of Mars
- Prepare for human exploration

TIME LINE OF MARS MISSIONS

1964–1965
Mariner 4 makes first successful flyby of Mars and sends back close-up images.

1969
Mariner 6 and *Mariner 7* flybys

1971–1972
Mariner 9 orbiter

1975–1982
Viking 1 orbiter and lander

1975–1980
Viking 2 orbiter and lander

1996–1997
Mars *Pathfinder* lander and *Sojourner* rover

1996–2006
Mars *Global Surveyor* orbiter

2001 to present
Mars *Odyssey* orbiter

2003 to present
Mars *Express* orbiter (*Beagle 2* lander lost on arrival)

GLOSSARY

APOLLO 11: the spaceflight mission that landed the first two humans (Americans Neil Armstrong and Buzz Aldrin) on the Moon on July 20, 1969

ATMOSPHERE: the gases that surround a planet

BACTERIA: single-celled organisms that live on, in, and around most living and nonliving things

BOOSTERS: the first stages of a rocket or spacecraft, which provide acceleration before they are jettisoned

EQUATOR: an imaginary line around a planet at an equal distance from its North Pole and its South Pole

GRAVITY: the force of attraction by which Earth and other massive objects pull other objects toward them

LIFE-SUPPORT SYSTEM: a group of devices that provides astronauts with oxygen while removing carbon dioxide and also typically includes water-cooling equipment, a fan, and a radio

ORBIT: a regular repeated course that one object takes around another object, such as Earth's orbit around the Sun

POWERED DESCENT VEHICLE: vehicle that fires retro-rockets to control and slow a rover's landing

RADAR: a device that sends out radio waves to detect the distance and location of objects

SOLAR SYSTEM: a group of planets orbiting a star; our solar system has eight planets

THRUSTER: a small rocket engine used to change a spacecraft's direction

UNIVERSE: all of space and everything in it

2003–2010	2003 to present	2005 to present	2007–2008	2011 to present	2013 to present	2013 to present	2016 to present
Mars exploration rover *Spirit* (landed 2004)	Mars exploration rover *Opportunity* (landed 2004)	Mars *Reconnaissance* orbiter	*Phoenix* Mars lander	Mars Science Laboratory rover *Curiosity* (landed 2012)	*MAVEN* probe	Mars Orbiter Mission	*ExoMars* orbiter